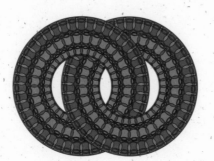

FUN BEING ME
Jack Wiler
POEMS

FUN BEING ME

Jack Wiler

POEMS

CavanKerry ❖ Press LTD.

Library of Congress Cataloging-in-Publication Data

Wiler, Jack.
Fun being me : poems / Jack Wiler. – 1st ed.
p. cm.
ISBN-13: 978-0-9723045-9-7
ISBN-10: 0-9723045-9-2
I. Title.

PS3573.I4286F86 2006
811'.6–dc22

2006017099

Cover art: "SIP" © Robert Piersanti, 2005
Cover and text design by Peter Cusack.

First Edition

Printed in the United States of America

CavanKerry Press Ltd.
Fort Lee, New Jersey
www.cavankerrypress.org

NOTABLE ⟡ VOICES

CavanKerry Press is proud to publish the works
of established poets of merit and distinction.

CavanKerry Press is grateful for the support it
receives from the New Jersey State Council on the Arts.

Acknowledgements

The following poems appeared in *Long Shot Magazine*:

"Homesick"
"Why Ask Why"
"Money Honey"
"I'm a Tourist"
"Letter to My Nieces"
"Cleaning House"

"Praying for Rest" appeared in the *Edison Literary Review*

"Mangoes & Rain" and "Bitteroot" appeared in *Omega* from Howling Dog Press

"Ways to Die" appeared in *Entelechy International: A Journal of Contemporary Ideas*

Thanks:
Many thanks to Joan Handler, Danny Shot, Jim Haba, Don Sheehan, and Lisa Rhoades for helping me on the way.

Dedication

This book is dedicated to Johanna and to my family and my friends who all dragged me back into the world of the living. Without them, the story wouldn't have the ending it does. God bless you all and keep you in His hand.

Table of Contents

PART I

What I Have and What I Don't Have

I have a jar of pennies about a third full.
It's a gallon jar that used to hold
cheap red Italian wine.
I used it to make Sangria.
I used to have a dollar forty.
I had it till this morning.
I bought two newspapers
and a container of orange juice.
I had to dip into the pennies
for the juice.
When I made the sangria
I put in the dago red,
some cheap brandy,
the juice of two oranges, a lime, two lemons,
some oj, sugar, and a sliced apple.
I drank it last summer on one of the last hot days.
I have a bed and a chair and a desk and a computer.
I have a kitchen table that was an outdoor table.
I have glasses, three, and plates, a full serving for six.
It used to be for eight.
I have a mop.
I have a vacuum cleaner.
I have clothes but they're all dirty.
I have no way to clean them until I get more money.
I have a dog.
She's dirty and sleeping.
I have an apartment over a bar.
I have the roar of Palisade Ave in my living room.
I can watch the hookers on a Saturday night from my

front window.
I have no women in my life.
I have no friends in my life.
I sit in my room and watch the TV.
I have cable so I can watch good TV
but I get bored so I read
the newspapers.
I read three newspapers a day.
They tell me everything that happens everyday and
they tell it all the same.
Two of them use the same wire service
so I get to read the same
story twice.
I need glasses.
I can't afford them.
My license is suspended.
I can't pay to get it restored.
I have a job
but it doesn't pay me money.
I have a breeze blowing through my window.
You can smell a fire from someone's fireplace.
I can see the Empire State from my kitchen window.
I can see the World Trade Center from my kitchen window.
I can hear sirens everyday all day long
rushing to Christ Hospital.
Carrying the sick to be saved.
I cried for hours last night over what I didn't have.
I went to sleep so I wouldn't be hungry.
I have food but it's not enough.
I don't have a girl
or a couch
or a person to hold me late at night

or curtains to muffle the sirens
or rugs to damp the echoes through these empty rooms.
I have no sense of irony.
I have a dollar forty, or did until this morning.
I have a jar with a heap of pennies
sitting on the floor.
The sun streaming in.
My dog snoring on the linoleum.
The smell of bacon from my landlord's apartment.
Kids playing down the block.
You couldn't buy this.
You wouldn't want to.

Choices

When I got pneumonia,
first I was weak,
tired,
climbing stairs beyond me.
Then the world began to get
smaller.
It began as a black border,
like the iris of an old
silent film camera.
Every day it grew bigger
and the world I saw
became smaller
till at the last
it was just a pinpoint.

Then another world opened.
A world rich in hallucination.
Clear visions of angels
and shrouded demons and
guides from another place
waiting to usher me to
their world.
A world alternately dark and
filled with copulating familiars
or bright with unspoken joy
and all the time each
world whispering, pick me,
pick me,
and in that fevered space,

a human would now and
then appear to ask,
how are we today?
We're fine but we are
choosing not to choose
death today
if you please.

Directions

This girl in the park is retarded.
All bundled up in down and wool
and wearing fuzzy white gloves and a huge grin
and she's spinning her hands like a top.
Waving and waving to everyone,
to no one,
to me, driving by in my car on the way to work.
She's got eyes filled with glory.
She's staring first at the New York skyline,
then at me and her gloves are spinning,
happy and mad.
I almost stop.
I almost think this is a warning.
But it's 8:45 and I'm late and the sun is up.
The traffic whirring into New York.
The news radio saying go slow;
the ice on the roads or snow,
and it's only November.
Go slow.
Watch out.
My boss just back from Florida.
My sales down for the second month in a row.
My dog scratching herself silly
with hot spots,
and gloves whirring happy and mad.
Sun glinting through the trees,
light with last leaves.
Warning.
My friend Andy says:

Pozor.
My friend Andy says:
You have to commit.
You have to see the truth in you to see the truth in others.
I'm doomed.
That's what my horoscope said.
Doomed in love, doomed to drive to work.
Doomed to watch over and over
the same TV shows, the same wars.
Saddam Hussein.
Jews.
Atom bombs.
Mangled children with white gloves and new dresses stacked up in
ditches in Bosnia.
I'm doomed and I'm really happy.
Happy to have this drive, happy to say hello
to this wretched little mad girl.
So I'd like to stop and say hello
but I don't and you don't have to either.
She's crazy.
New York is crazy.
My sister's so sad sometimes
she can't get out of bed but what the fuck,
this little girl is on a bench looking
at the crashed New York stock market,
the $2000 dollar a month apartments,
the men shoving shopping carts loaded with thousands
of 7 UP cans and she's waving.
She's saying:
go on, it's ok.
Go on.
So I do.

Write About Your Illness

That's what you should do.
This is a friend talking.
A well intentioned, decent woman.
I like her so I consider her request.
Seriously.
But I would prefer not to say.
After all it's over and I'm
well.
But she insists.
Insists.

So, here is a way to think
about my illness:
think about it like a winter storm.
First it's just weeks of cold and
gloom.
Vague stories in the press,
worried friends, half-hearted
attempts at preparation.

Then it sweeps in and it isn't
a storm; it's a blizzard
that lasts for days.
You are left alone, quiet,
and weak in the middle
of white and wind and worry.
When will it end?
Will it never stop snowing?

Then it does.
It stops snowing and you
start to move out
slow through huge drifts.
Weak from the effort.
Then the snow is ice and then deep black heaps of
garbage
and dog shit
and what took three days
to fall lingers for a month.

The sun comes out but it's cold.
It could snow again at anytime
and it does, a flurry, a couple inches.
And then like some little miracle,
it's spring and sunny and warm,
except deep inside, you're
still chilled to the bone.
You look in the mirror
and you see a frozen ghost.
Then people want to know about
being sick
but who wants to talk about ghosts, who wants to look
under his skin to see the winter
growing somewhere far away?
Not me.
So here's another way to talk
about my disease, my best
friend, my curse, my salvation,
my stigmata;
it's a time of vomit
and shit and fever and sick smells

and parents who hate your
lazy guts and it's the time
I was a skeleton.
It wasn't a storm;
it wasn't a trial;
it was a long time spent
with death and all things
being equal,
I much prefer to avoid the mirror.

Bitterroot

It's not like you can't buy gas if you want it.
It's not like there aren't any gas stations.
Like Iraq had won and we're all wearing towels.
It's not that cars don't litter the highway.
That the squeal of tires doesn't fill the early morning,
the roar of trucks gearing down,
the thick funk of diesel fuel in the gutters.
It's just that I can't buy gas!
That my car has been repossessed.
That my life is spent in old buses.
My gas card is cancelled.
My front headlamp dims when I hit the security button
on my key chain; there's no reassuring bleat of the horn
telling me my car is waiting for me in the dark
when I leave for my new job.
Instead I trudge down to the corner
to wait for the public transportation.
As if buses built this country.
As if Lewis and Clark took the number 84 up into the Bitterroots.
The 84 to the Bitterroots!
If they'd of had a car, it would have been a big one.
Rear end slamming off the guard rails.
Radio loud.
Sun slamming off the rims.
Hands slamming the wheel to the sounds of border radio.
Loud.
Big.
America.
And they'd have had a gas card!

They'd have had a security system that worked.
Something to scare the crap out of the Indians
snuffling up around that big mother of a automobile.
And they'd have laughed when the little red
squints jumped.
Yeah, they'd have laughed and I bet they're laughing at me now.
Head down in the rain.
The bus passed me by and now I'm waiting
for the next 84 to Fairview and every girl that walks by
looks at me like I'm old and stupid and like a guy whose car
is gone whose radio broke or if it works just gets
talk radio one o one point what the fuck all and
has to listen to two old guys babbling about
Bob Dole or Iraq
or the way the economy is run by the Jews
and the only good thing about the bus
is that there's no radio at all.
Like what it was like when Lewis and Clark
went walking up into the Bitterrroots all quiet
and cold and alone and you could just hunch over
on your horse and it would all just run over you,
the sky, the sun, the things you left, the things you dreamed.
They were all gone and it was just you,
walking real slow up a hard, high hill.

The Last Church in Jersey City

My friend Sarge sat in a tree for a year once.
He made it up just like a treefort.
High, high in the night forest.
Every evening he would look up and see the stars.
Constellations whose name he'd never been taught.
This was 1968 or 1969.
In the morning without fail, he'd roll a joint,
clean his gun and shoot tiny people.
Frail arms, slender hands,
huge red eruptions of blood at the back of their heads.

The last church in Jersey City
has it's pews in a backyard.
It's altar tipped over.
It's poor box ripped open.
When you leave, you notice a squirrel
drinking holy water.
The seven worshippers who arrive each Saturday
arrive so they can sleep late Sunday.
There is no priest, no altar boys, no hymns.

Marc Parent would organize his stockroom
with an intense fervor.
Everything stacked and labeled by
size, purpose and expiration.
He'd learned in the Navy
how to fix torpedos.
How to sequence them so they'd
rise from their beds in the sea, quiet.

Roar out and up to the sky
and on a bad, bad day crash to the ground.
When Marc got cancer he called to his Lord
to save him.
He asked for health and he didn't die.

I walk past the last church in Jersey City each day.
I have thirteen cents in my pockets.
My hair is dirty and uncut and I beg for money.
I usually get it from someone.
I sit in bars and listen to my friends saying,
no, praying,
no,
begging
for the ball to clear the fence.
Home run.
For the shot to drop.
Three points.
The putt to break left.
Now.

It's a miracle when it does.
When the clack clack of the Western Union printer
gives me some small check.
Some little hope, forty bucks here,
a hundred there.
It's a miracle
that I find eggs at a buck for two dozen.
That I find the last six dollar bottle of wine.
That I can look up and remember
the names of that cluster of stars.
They're the seven sisters.
Thank God, they're still there.

The Lives of Women

She's in the basement, crying.
All she can smell is mold and bleach and detergent.
She's sick to her stomach with a flu.
She thinks about the ocean and the salt drying on her skin
and the taste of clams.
She's crying and she feels the house shake
when a train rumbles through the town.
She likes the sound of the walls rattling.
She can have any man she wants in the bar after two drinks.
She can.
She likes it when she comes by surprise.
When she's making love and it just comes up and takes her.
She can hear her children outside.
She can hear their arguments.
That's not fair.
She's not scared, not really.
She can smell the damp wood near the sump pump.
She burrows her head in a pair of jeans and
smells the sweat of her husband.
It's late in March and she wishes she could stop crying,
wishes she were in a bar with a glass of cold vodka
listening to the high laugh of a drunk two seats down.
There's a dark angel at her door.
It's knocking and knocking and knocking and
it's loud, then it's soft, but it never stops.
Oh God, she wishes it were April and she wishes she were dead
and she wishes she were alive and happy and the dark angel
would be gone.

Belief Systems

I don't believe in God but
I believe in you.
I believe the world spins
and that if you step on a crack
you break your mother's back.
I believe I broke my mother's heart
when I left my wife and
that there was a crack in the world
that I fell in when my mother died.
I believe if you find a penny
and pick it up
that all the day you'll have good luck.
I believe that this is a sad, sad world.
That men pushing shopping carts loaded
up with 7 UP cans is not
good.
That I have been a cruel and selfish
fool and that if God could see,
if He could reach out,
He would touch me.
And I believe the touch of God
is the rough heave of waves
on a thousand storm tossed seas.
I believe the gold spire of NY Life
is wrapped in dense fall clouds.
That taxis come and go and try
as I might I can't
make them stop for me.
This world of loss.

Of cracks stepped on so often
the mother of God
can't stop weeping.
I believe I've stepped on a crack.
I believe I'm wrong
too often and I believe
I've got a long walk home from here.
I believe that I believe
in too little too late and
that somewhere in New York City
you can walk on a street that's lit
just a little by that light from that
huge golden spire.
I believe that's you walking down that street.
I believe that I'm lost
and it's dark.

How We Know We're Sick

You're walking down Franklin St.
in Jersey City on a hot summer
day and you have twenty dollars
and a bottle of wine and some groceries and you fart but
instead you shit your pants
for what seems like an hour
and remember it's a hot
summer day so you're wearing
shorts and the shit
runs down your legs in
brown ribbons just like
with Greta Waitz in the
New York Marathon but
this,
this is no marathon.
Just a river of shit you
jumped into and now you
can't get out. Waddling
in the brown current,
embarrassed though
no one sees,
at least, not yet.
This is being really sick
but also really stupid,
crying on a summer day
when you shit yourself
and no one saw.
No one but you,
sick little shit covered beast.
All alone under
a remorseless summer sun.

PART II

Chance in all Its Forms

Chance bites Karen's inner thigh.
Way up high
where she won't show me.
I pass her three times in the hall.
Each time her shoulders are bare,
her hair loose, wet.
She's older than me, maybe fifty six or so.

I'm on the phone.
Could be a business call.
I hang it up.
Pause.
Don walks by,
takes my face in his hands and
kisses the top of my head.

Peg is barely even a person.
Cancer took her teeth and her tits and
she's whacked on morphine and shitty wine.
She leans into me for a hug
and kisses my neck.
Wet and thick, like a lover.

I ate a perfect meal last night.
Chicken, arugula salad, and fingerling potatoes.
I had a bottle of ungodly wine from California.
The moon was full and sweet.
Blessings come and I never even know it.

Things I Can't Say at East Brunswick High School

First, I can't say fuck.

And I can't say motherfucker obviously and it would probably go without say-
ing that I can't say fuck you but it occurs to me at times that fuck you is what
a lot of people think when they're in school but you can't say it. At least not
out loud and not in a poem and not in front of a classroom of children. I could
probably talk about whether they're children or not. But I can't tell them to fuck
off. Although the people that tell me what I can and can't say clearly want to
be able to tell the children to fuck off or at the very least they'd like their par-
ents to eat shit. I can't say that either. Eat shit. Or suck my dick. No way they'd
let me call them cocksuckers but they are. Cocksuckers. They're also shitheads
and assholes and mealy mouthed little pissants. I might be allowed to say pis-
sants. Maybe not. It's got piss in it. You'd think their teachers would want to
get up one day and walk into a classroom and tell all the little shitheads with
their bmw's and suv's and rich mom's and dads to fuck off but they don't and
they won't let me, so fuck em. I can't say pussy. I can't say cunt. I can't say
faggot. Or queer or cocksucker but I already went over that didn't I? The kids
can call each other queers and the teachers can bitch about the little faggots
and they can all laugh when little Jimmy in the band gets his ass kicked but
they can't say it out loud. They can just think it. Or talk among themselves.

This is high school.

And since it's high school every fucking one of them has to pretend that noth-
ing happens outside their door. They have to act like mommy and daddy are
nice and the kids are okay and it's a good idea to invade various small coun-
tries and the best way to get along is go along and so we can't have any
fucking queer, poet, shithead going around saying cunt in front of the kids
because god knows where that would lead.

It's fucking nuts.

But it's exactly what you'd expect in America although you'd expect it was nineteen fucking fifty fucking nine and not two thousand and three you know? It's mother fucking astounding that thirty years after I got out of this shit it's still exactly the fucking same. Nice clean kids sitting in rows all listening to nice teachers talking about some version of history where nobody does anything but work to raise up his kids and grow old and die happy in bed surrounded by his smiling children and I hope you're noticing I'm not even putting a woman in all of this nor is anybody in this little scenario black or Chinese or Indian or anything other than white, white, white to the tippy toes of their fucking little white feet. I think I could say almost all of this and get a little rise out of the attendant students and teachers if I left out the fucking little white feet.

So let's be clear.

I can't say fuck in East Brunswick New Jersey in the poetry classroom while pretending to be an expert on poetry in front of a culturally diverse group of students who come here out of some sense of duty and a legal obligation who are overseen in this activity by underpaid employees of the state who while they may have some ideas of educating the children they teach are basically tired of them and who are in turn overseen by even more underpaid employees and all so that they will learn the essentials of American culture and history and when it's done they all go home to eat and worry and work but the one thing they can't do in this place, this classroom, this school, is to say anything that reflects the fucking world they actually live in because that's a bad, bad thing to do. It's a really bad, bad thing. So fuck them and fuck this school and God bless fucking America.

Money Honey

I work on the river in New Jersey.
From my window I can see New York
and the harbor and the river and the huge buildings
that make it New York.
And it's all money.
It's the World Financial Center.
It's Wall Street.
It's the rent.
It's the receptionist and the nice hotels
and the strip joints and cigars and brandy.
And it's money.
And it's poetry.
Ok, not poetry that you expect,
money shouldn't be poetry, right?
Poetry should be glory and honor and joy.
But if I sell my book or my cd or my vision
I get money.

I read about John Singer Sargent.
He painted people with money
and they gave him money and everyone
hates what he did because he got money.
He made a bunch of money and got fat and happy
and in the article I read, everybody hated his guts for it.

I live over a bar,
Little One's,
and from my kitchen I can see Manhattan
and the river of money

and I want the money.
I want to write poems someone would pay for.

They never do.
So what the fuck does it matter if I get paid or not.
I can see the river; I can taste the money.
I can write about the money roiling under the river.
I can watch it crest the banks and break on the shores,
hard waves of money.
I can taste it and smell it and it's all money.
It's all green and pure and real and even if it's just
tulips in Holland in the sixteenth century that
some fool pays ten thousand dollars for,
red and brilliant and blooming in a country
that should be under water,
it's money that I should have because
I understand the river.
I know the smell of money.
Its glory, its honor, its richness.
Its women with pure alabaster skin,
the olive texture you can almost taste.
So who cares if we write for money,
or for glory,
or for honor,
or for art,
or for some fool who thinks art runs the world.
Because the world runs on something else.
Not money.
Not glory.
Not honor.
Not joy.
Not decency.

Not fun.
The world runs on an engine
the world doesn't even know is there.

It's like you were given a car and you lived in some
little Polynesian island and you never had seen a car.
And you put a key in it and it rears up
with a great and fearful roar.
It's God.
It's a tulip.
It's the most fearsome engine you'd ever seen or heard.
It's money.
It's love.
It's the way your mother's kiss felt.
It's the way the sky smells before snow.
It's flying fish leaping in the dawn sun.
It's the way your girl smelled after you fucked her.
So you say, "How many shells, how many perfect shells,
does this cost?"
And God says,
"It costs more than you'll ever have but I can help you get it."
And the next thing you know, you're a salesman.
You know if you can show someone that they need a perfect shell,
a red tulip,
a dollar with a picture of George Washington,
then you can understand why Manhattan is gorgeous
at 11PM on a Thursday night in January.
Then you'll know why
we get out of bed all over the world.
Why we all speak English.
Why shells give us the grand design of the universe.

It's money.
It's not that big of a deal.
It's a river.
It's a river with canoes loaded with gunpowder and iron and words
and if you can't talk, you can't sell.
And if you can't sell, you can't get any money.
And if you can't get any money, you
can't buy a red tulip
in January in New York
to give your girl
and the sad, sad truth is that your girl doesn't
want a red tulip.
She wants you
or that river of money or
red tulips rising with angry joy
every morning like a tide washing up dozens of perfect shells.
And we all walk the beach hoping to find the design of the shell
that brings us the money that will let us get the girl,
the new house,
the respect,
the flower in the vase in the house
in the riverfront apartment.
It's a glorious, joyous, clamorous, mad whirl and when
you're done, you're in Manhattan counting the dollars
in your wallet and there never seem to be enough,
but what the fuck, it's only money and it's never enough.

Like I Was

I'm almost like I was before.
Almost like it was six years ago
when I had a home and I was in love.
My nice car. My garden.
My suits that fit so nice.
Almost like that,
like I was.
Like I didn't almost die.
Like I never saw the dark man standing outside.
Waiting for me at the corner.
Like those towers didn't fall
and I still had my dog
and my muscles weren't eaten
by bacteria that looked
like fish eggs.
Hungry like children
always eating.
Always hungry,
like I wasn't there, like I was food.
Like you can watch fire in the tower and
listen to millions of hungry children
and the chatter of nurses and guns whispering.
They whisper and whisper.
But I'm not like I was.
I'm tired and hungry.
Eating all the day, watching TV,
the towers in flames everyday.
I'm not like I was.
I was dead
and now I'm not.

Running the River

Let's suppose it's 1989
and I meet you for the first time.
You say your name.
Meg Kearney
and I think about
Kearny, NJ and the Passaic River
and the smooth run of sculls up
and down the river.
The boatswain's cry of
pull.
Let's suppose the pull of oar
against brown water,
is the pull of two people, me and you,
and I say, I'm so happy to meet you
and the oar comes out smooth,
then dips and pulls hard.
Then, maybe I'm on a bridge
over the river watching single sculls
and I see you, sweat
on your forehead, your shoulders.
Then I fall in love
over nothing,
over sweat, oars dip and rise,
deep hard pulls.

This is like a time machine.
This moment when we kiss.
The drip of river on river
and I say, hello, and I say nothing

of purpose but
I own the river.
I own the oar.
I know everything about the oarsman.
I say, stop.
Stop the race.

I say, I love her.
The judges are pissed.
The boats slide into muddy banks and
old, discarded tires and the river is on fire.

That's how it should have been.

There should have been quiet.
The judges put down their pencils.
The oarsmen put up their oars,
you stand up tall
in a slender vessel
and both of us know it won't founder.
You say, hello, it's a pleasure to meet you.
Newark burns to the ground.
Kearny lights up with wild, crazy fire.
The wild Oompampanoosuc
runs over its banks
and each of us knows the race is run.

But not in this world.
In this world
I'm a stupid fuck.
In this world
you fall in love again and again

and I watch tv.
But tonight when I turn on the TV
it's the all rowing network.
It's all oars dipping in
the wild Oompompanoosuc.
It's crazy, it's now, it's me being
a desperate fool,
writing over and over and over
about single sculls, about
rivers running through Kearny and
they're all on fire.

It's late, it's 1998, it's the apocalypse.
It's not too late.
I'm pleased to make your acquaintance.

Clouds at Night

I'm drunk and it's midnight or two or 11:30
and everyone's asleep.
Except me.
I walk out into the field and
spin around, drink in hand, and I always say,
always,
look at all the fucking stars.
The first time I saw them Peter and I and Debbie Boe
were walking home on the highway to Easton.
For August it was cold,
like winter, and we lay on our backs
in the road and the Milky Way
ran on forever and the Perseids
rained down on us.
I read today about the Perseids.
Clouds of dirt and gas,
basically shit being spat out of some
blown up comet.
The something or other Tuttle Comet.
Tuttle, like some old guy
working for some smart ass young guy
thinks he knows it all.
Tuttle's young boss lords it over him.
Throws him a couple bones.
A trip to Chicago.
A bucket of balls at the driving range.
But with each thwack of his
Big Bertha Tuttle's boss
thinks, adios you stupid fuck.

and Tuttle must shit three times
every morning just thinking about work.
Plop
and plop and
plop.
He's fucked.
So we get gorgeous rains of light
on a cold August night and I think
all this might mean God is watching.
Not well or close,
but watching.

Hell

I go out drinking with Jessica and her friends.
We shoot pool.
I shoot great pool.
All my shots drop.
Jess's friend Jane shoots with me.
She sucks.
But even her dumbest shot drops and I win
and I lose.
Go figure.
I'm in love with a woman who's married.
I don't know what to do.

So I go out drinking with Jessica and her friends
and I shoot pool and I win.
Eight ball in the corner off two rails
and it drops.
Even on a table where the rails are so dead nothing
comes off them.
Shots you could die for.
The gorgeous babe in the corner comes up to me and
shakes my hand and leans over and kisses me gently
and it's all because I can't miss.
My beer tastes like stale soap.
I'm hungry and the bar doesn't serve food.
I can't miss and I can't go home with Jess.
I'd trade every solid in every side pocket for one long kiss.
It doesn't happen.
Never wish for what you want.
When it comes it's not what you expected.

It's sad and glorious and it's empty of joy.
She looks away and her shoulder is momentarily bare.
Just a black bra strap.
And the hint of lipstick on her lips
is so far away I can never taste it.
I shoot perfect pool.
I'm everybody's friend.
I'm the perfect escort.
I'm the chump who gets on the train to Jersey
by himself, who gets in the cab by himself.
The man who wants what he can't have
and never will.

God woke up last Thursday and looked around
for ways to fuck with me and this is what He came up with.
Jack will shoot perfect pool.
He'll spend the night with Jessica and her friends.
He'll never be happy and she'll never love him.
You'd think a Supreme Being would have better things to do.

Sick of Being Sick

I was lying on my back for a month, oh I would get up
to piss or puke, but I mostly
lay and watched tv and
slept and ate.
A skeleton draped with
a ready-made shroud.

Then I began to move about.
To stir as it were in the world.
I might sit in my little white chair
in the shower or move
out to the living room
to receive a reluctant guest
or shuffle out to the
van from the AIDS center
to see a doctor or a nurse.

Then one night full of
spit and vinegar, I ventured
out for soda on a cold
January night and saw the rich
swirl of stars and dizzy
with joy fell and split my head
and out came everything I
used to care about:
shoes and sweaters and dinners in
New York and girlfriends and
boyfriends and they ran red
and steamed on the frozen

snow and I almost couldn't rise.
The skeleton of a whale washed
up on a distant shore surrounded
by kelp and whale puke.

But rise I did and walk I did
and out of the mouth of the
beast, the great whale came I,
simple, hardworking, a God-
fearing man with his head
bowed under the weight
of stars, the retch of life.

We're All Going to the Lake

We're going to the lake!
All of us.
We're loading up the minivans.
We're slapping up the kickstands.
We're running around the house,
screaming about how we can't
find our badges or our high band
or our favorite suit.
Which was right here and
we're getting up slow from lunch
and walking out to the car.
We're going to the lake!
Eight housewives, twenty five kids,
three lifeguards, one kid in the refreshment stand to dish up the water ice,
me and once in a while a dad and maybe some teenagers,
who are loud and look scary but
swim like shit once they hit the water
and smack!
What a lake to dive into!
A long brown ribbon of cedar water.
Trees brushing it's sides, bright blue skies
fill it with clouds
and turtles strung out on a log.
They're so tired from this hot, hot sun they forget to eat.
So the crappies and minnows
are all over the shallows.
Gotta get while the getting's good.
Far, far out on the lake a big bass leaps up, flops down
and nobody sees the water ripple out.

They're riding their bikes
down Jefferson or Monroe.
Towels over their shoulders
snapping in the rush.
A whine of spokes and muscle that's been going on for fifty years.
Fifty years of kids hauling their
bodies trawling streams of brown water,
small muscles stretched,
yelling, running, tight little balls that
cannon into the water!
O Joy! O headlong rush to water!
O the whir of spokes!
The shrieks!
The gossip!
The affairs.
Bodies lying in beds, dreaming of other
bodies last night, last week.
Husbands, lovers.
Heat raising tiny beads of sweat,
the bathing suit tossed heedless on the chair.
The brush of finger to breast.
The wives dreaming of sweat;
muscled backs, thick bellies.
The drop falling from his chin,
running down her breast.
But then the kids are yelling!
We gotta go swimming!
Insistent!
Water calling water.
Awkward crawl
head out of water
crazy seven-year-old treading water.

mad dog paddle.
Mom watching, feet in water,
not really there,
but cool and wet on a hot, hot day.
O Wenonah Lake!
Canoes, boats, rafts,
big fat guy, belly up,
floating.
The only husband here today.
Me, watching housewives,
watching kids
splashing Dad,
slap of hand on water.
Ripples that go all the way to shore.
We're all at the lake!
We've brought everything we need.
Life jackets, blankets, sunscreen, towels, badges, bands,
balls, rubber killer whales, sunhats, sun glasses, coolers,
cocktails cleverly disguised as lemonade, water,
watches, buckets to carry water and
desire.
All for the lake!
On a hot, hot day.
We go to the lake for the water.
Come in!
Come in!
Come in!

Circuit Breakers

Her brother, eighteen, leaned
up out of the pool reaching for a volleyball.
His hand caught a live wire.
Pulled the plug on the whole family.
Now every Sunday they come together
and it's no Mass they celebrate.
It's that leap to the wire and
the moment of disconnect that
pulls them back.
Come Sunday they all return to the stoop.
Everyone to his place.
Father seated at the center,
just through the door about to call for dinner.
One sister two doors down with a
girlfriend talking about boys.
The other crossing the street
a little stoned, her hair wet from
swimming.
The older brothers are at the top of the stoop
smoking cigarettes, drinking beers.
She is in her car pulling away fifteen minutes earlier.
She is in her car pulling up an hour later.
The hand of the youngest brother is reaching.
Its fingers ready to tighten.
Pull the wire,
miss the ball,
draw them back,
suck them away.
Start the circuit.

Dark Matters

I have a friend who has a second home.
He goes to his home on a boat, a little boat, with a little engine.
The home is on an island.
It's a small island, on a small lake in New Hampshire.

My friend is an engineer.
He became an engineer to prove the existence of God.
He studied dark matter.
He married and bought the house on the island and
every weekend went to the house on the island to make it better.

If you gave him a black box and told him it showed the existence
of God, he'd ask how and try to make it better.
He'd try to make it show God in all Her myriad forms.
Make God dance across the waves.
Make God swim like a bass in dark water.
Make God piss outside and bathe in cold water.
He'd say the box could do much more
but he'd never just look at the box.
He'd never see what God is.

I have a friend who's a salesman.
If you told him you had a black box that showed the existence of God,
he'd ask how much money you could get for that.
He'd charge this and he'd charge that but he could
give a fuck about what it's worth to know about the existence of God.
Just how much he could get and when he got it, he'd want more.

I have a friend who lives on a lake in a town in Vermont.
He knows God.
I'm not sure if he's met Him or not but it seems like he has.
His kids drive him nuts.
They get married; they get divorced; they drink; they're kids.

All my friends study dark matter and none of them learn shit.
God wakes up and looks around and has better things to do.
She eats a good breakfast and lies around by the pool at the Delano in
        Miami Beach.
She likes guys with tight abs and She likes a well made martini.
She's especially happy when a storm sweeps through the Caribbean and
takes out a dozen small towns.
It's Her job.
It's dark and it matters.
It's Her life.
Give Her a box and She knows what to do with it.
Fill it up and empty it out.
Cost is no object.
The little boat on the lake on a calm day sputtering along.
That's Her job.
The man's marriage collapsing because he drinks or fools around.
That's Her job.
The cable outage, the phone that dies, the moment when you
come with a great cry.
Her job.
God could give a fuck about dark matter or a great sale or how much
        money
you make.

Darkness matters.
The distant rumble of thunder,

that matters.

The little laugh in her sleep when your wife is dreaming,

that matters.

The taste of bad chicken or the smell of a deep swamp or the deep roar of
the crowd at a sporting event, they matter.

All the rest is vanity

and that matters too.

PART III

Dream at the Gate to Hell

There's the head of a child gone to rot.
Mouth wide.
Staked to the ground.

There's a stream in summer
filled with floating turtles.
They snap and pull
when they brush my legs.

There are sounds.
The boom, boom of a manhole cover
each time a car drives over.
It's sweet and deep on a hot night.
The whisper of fans.
The buses gearing up.
The drivers leaning on their horns
for the drunk guy in the '82 Mazda to move his car.
Move his fucking car.

And my dog snoring, loud,
keeping me safe on a summer night.
Big, black, Rottweiler,
happy, sleeping, telling everyone she's there.
I'm safe.
She's a warning.
Like the gong striking outside a Chinese temple.
Like the geese swarming toward an intruder,
honking and honking.

Like that hideous thing staked in front of a snowy field.
A child's head.
Screaming.
Its mouth filled with snow.

Spring at Little One's

I walked out into a field last weekend in Clinton, New Jersey.
It was cold and the ground was frozen,
crisp and hard and cracking when you walked
and up above was Orion.
In New Jersey.
Stars.
Not millions but enough.
Orion and his belt and the whole universe spinning around them
and me in a field with two happy dogs.
At home was my dog
all scratchy with allergies
and downstairs Little One's Bar
with salsa pounding or merinque pounding
and happy girls screaming on the street,
saying, everybody will think we're lesbians.
But I don't.
I think they're happy.
I think I'm upstairs in my room
with my scratchy dog
thinking about the stars spinning all around me.
Thinking this is a message and the message is
get the fuck out of bed, go for a walk.
Watch the stars.
Eat good food.
Enjoy the shoes on your feet.
Listen to your friends talk.
Watch your friends Danny and Caroline talk to their kids.
Talk about star wars and power rangers
and fighting with light swords

while they drive their space ships straight to the stars.
We should all be in that ship.
We're not.
Most of us are going to work
in Dodge Neons or old broken down Toyotas
and when we get to work we don't say hello to anyone.
We don't know what we're doing or why we do it.
I sell a box that derives signals from satellites and
the signals tell you where your Dodge Neon's been and where it's going
and it says how fast you go and
how slow you go and when you stop
and on the map printout it shows it all in color
and you can print it out on an inkjet and its kind of pretty
and if you're boss reads it out you're fired.
Then you don't have a Dodge Neon.
You're living over Little One's
drinking cheap wine and bemoaning your fate.
I'm like a tiny god.
So because of that I figure God's not a happy man.
He's up just beyond Orion drinking a glass of good champagne
that tastes a little sour.
He's had way too much.
Everybody looks tiny to him.
Nobody comes to visit.
That's God.
God should have a party.
Invite us all in.
Show us the lights and the fun and ask us to enjoy it.
Instead He's always fiddling with the little shit.
Inventing microbes and software and sorrow.
We're all sick in our houses with bad winter colds and hoping spring
will come.

That's His job too.
Making spring.
He's a little late this year.
Maybe He's hungover.
New Year's dragged on a little longer than He hoped.
You notice I think God's a man.
He'd have to be because He's never satisfied.
He's got spring and summer and fall and winter and Orion
and the cosmos and He still feels the need to fuck shit up
with war and sorrow and making something really stupid happen
like Bosnia.
So tonight I'm thinking I'll help him out.
I'm going to pretend I believe spring is on the way.
I'm going to pretend I'll find a girl.
I'm going to pretend that being sad or angry or foolish is a stupid
thing to do and I'm going to be happy.

Getting Better

It's not like a game.
Although my brother seemed
to think it was.
You've got to walk,
he'd say, and walk I would.
Or he'd insist I lift
weights so we bought
a set of dumbbells.

But it seems that these
were all just games themselves.
Just ways to fool
each other into believing
that by dint of hard work
and training, I'd improve.
Instead the weights
disfigured & crippled me
and the walking stripped
away my precious pounds.

What I needed was patience
and prayer and food and
the knowledge I would
always be sick.
In fact,
I always had been sick.
All of us are.
Every day the body
a battleground:

germs, viruses, microbes
without measure
lining up to assault
the corrupt and doomed
husk of flesh.
Every day we are sick,
sick and tired and worn.

Each day we pick up our
burdens knowing we
walk hand in hand with death.

Glory

I'm out driving with my friends.
We're driving down US 1 from Russian River.
We've been to several wineries
and I've had six great wines
and several bad wines.
It's a beautiful day in a beautiful land.
The red wine I can't taste
because I've lost my sense of smell.
Then, at one winery, we're offered a Shiraz
That's so rich and deep,
it explodes in my nose and my mouth
and my head and I lean back and say
thank you.
Thank you for this wine,
for this day with my friends,
and then we leave.
So right here you'd think it all ends and
you'd be wrong.
Because right here it begins.
We drive down through the valley
and it's not all that impressive.
Then we wheel out to the coast
and God says,
take a look chump.
It's spread out all around.
Glory.
Like you'd never expect.
Sheer cliffs, sun glinting off beaches no one
should ever see.

Surf, rough and evil and scary.
I'm with my friends so all I say is "Oh my God"
but what I want to do is cry.
I'm crying now.
For beauty no one should ever see.
I'm from New Jersey.
The world is small and safe and it never brings
you to tears.
But then it never falls apart or burns or fills with sharks.
I'm reminded of Rilke,
"You must change your life,"
and of course I don't
and really no one here does either.
But they should.
They should wake up and realize that
if there is an argument for God
it's right here all around them.
Instead they drink good wine,
eat food so good you would
drive 100 miles to eat it.
I fly 3000 miles.
I read poems to people in a bay
that takes my breath away
and all I can think of is
God is one mean motherfucker.

Why I Love My Town

There are three good things about this town.
The first is you can hear the rain.
All the ways that rain can sound.
A slow clank on a metal porch roof.
A soft hum of a steady drizzle.
Hard huge drops that slap against everything.
Rain that doesn't come but suggests itself
in thunderheads a dozen miles away.

The second is that it has a fire whistle.
You still hear the sirens of police cars and fire trucks,
not as many as in a city but the same clamor and nervous jitter.
You can hear them a long way off.
The next town over maybe or two towns away
and then they're rushing by your house
and then they're fading, fading.
But better than the sirens is the whistle.
So big it fills the night when it goes off.
If you're watching television you can't hear
your show, just a loud, loud roar of the whistle
calling all the volunteer firemen to come put out a fire.
Or telling you there's a horrible disaster.
Or telling all the kids in town to go home.
Or telling you it's time for the parade on the 4th of July
and you have no idea which is which.
It's just loud and if you're on the phone
people say what's that noise?
What's that really loud noise?
You say, it's the fire whistle and they say,

why is it so loud?
And you say, so everyone knows there's a disaster.
You say, so everyone knows they should be home
doing homework or walking to the main street to watch
the veterans marching by and the flags.
You say, it's loud so you can't hear the TV,
you say, it's better than a telephone; everyone can hear it
and you know it's a lie.
They can't.
Everyone can't hear it anymore than they can hear the sirens two towns
away wailing late into the night.
We've got our doors closed, our windows down, the AC cranked high.
We're screaming at the kids;
we're drunk; we're asleep in our beds.
We don't know about the troubles screaming through the night.
We don't know the kids are drunk, that our homes are on fire,
our mother is dead in her chair for almost half an hour; her
cigarette has caught the house on fire and we don't know.
We don't know the buildings have fallen.
We don't know firemen are already dead.
We don't know; we don't care; we don't want to know and
this whistle is an abomination.
It's a loud godawful signal from somewhere far away that
we all wish would stop
so we can go back to our puzzle,
our shows,
our sad lives,
and our nice houses, in a nice town and I'm already
thinking of going to the next council meeting
to complain to have it turned off.
We could reach everyone by cell, by pager, by phone.
We don't need the whistle.

It's old fashioned.
It's loud.
It won't be quiet.
It won't let us sleep.
And sleep is what we need and that's why I like this town.
Because everyone is asleep and they cherish their silence.

When I was ten, I thought the whistle was to tell us the Russians
were going to drop the A bomb. That's what I think it's really for.
That's the third thing I like about this town.
Just before we all die, we'll hear three one minute blasts on the fire whistle.

Homesick

This town we live in is just one long siren.
Just one big traffic light and it never changes.
People here don't speak English.
The gas stations are all out of gas.
The cops are all on the take.
This town stinks.
This town's always on fire
or a fire's almost always just about out and
the smell of it ruins your breakfast.
This town has two streets and they both go the same way.
Straight to hell.
But you never get there because the light's busted a block away
or somebody's double parked
or turning left or there's a bus in front of you
that never moves.
Everybody's a junkie in this town
and they're all getting off that bus.
Nobody has exact change.
Everybody's a junkie or old or selling something to old junkies or
else they're cops driving around with their siren stuck and
the old junkies lean out the windows to
watch the cars
sitting in traffic.

Company Picnic

I hate dreams with my mother in them.
Like this one.
Not only does it have my mother,
it has the monsters in the ground.
Sometimes they're skeletons
or hands or vampires but
that doesn't matter, they're
in the ground and I can call them up
by banging on the ground
and I always do.

There's a dead kid.
He's a junkie but he's been dead in the bathroom
for what looks like a week and he's only got one leg
and you can see the mechanics of his fake leg
through his rotting blue trousers.
The blue tiled bathroom goes on forever,
showers and tubs and steamrooms
and mold on everything.

The dream began with me at a picnic.
I'm with some guy who's interviewing me for a job.
I get a turkey sandwich like they make in a deli and put it on a table
and go back to get a coke and then it all begins.
My mom calling me asking me where the car keys are
and she's got the same horrible page boy
haircut she had when she died and she's hounding
me for the keys and I'm really hungry
running around looking for a coke

and I hear the ground thudding like something's inside,
something that wants to come out,
some bones.
And I hide in the blue bathroom
and sit in a stall and look down and see the dead kid.

Really, I'm just hungry.
I don't need this dead kid.
I don't need my mom calling me.
I just want a coke and a pickle
to go with my sandwich.
Then the picnic's over and I still haven't
gotten to eat.

I don't want to interview for a job.
Answer questions I'd rather not answer.
Talk to someone I detest with a smile on my face.
I hate missing my mother.
It's been a really long, long time.
She should be gone for good.
I hate bones that live in the ground and don't come out.
But we go down.
We go down.
I hate that too.

Poetry for Fun and Profit

Hal is kind of pasty faced, like he's having cold sweats
and when he reads it's the same two poems.
His hair's cut nice though
and his clothes look good.
Andy's mad at me.
Not using the mike, maybe too full of myself.
I'm staring at Genie Morrow like I'm ten
and I feel stupid.
But when she sings, her eyes go up and back,
and when I tell Caroline about this,
that it's ecstatic,
like religious,
Andy overhears and tells me I'm a complete fool.
Or maybe it was Jackie.
Either way I feel dumb.
So I stop talking.
For about two minutes.
Then I'm calling Barbara, Babs, which she clearly hates
and if I had any insight,
I'd tell her how gorgeous she is
after, what, fifteen years.
But instead I'm chattering on and on,
drinking brandy after brandy to cure my cold.
I think about Sherry
telling me I'm like a ten year old, his hand way up,
bouncing up and down,
pick me, pick me.
Bab's! Genie! Sherry!
Listen to me!

I'm one funny guy,
and cute too,

Well, maybe they're right.
Tonight my act's dying
and I'm talking to Frank,
the drummer in Rob and Jackie's new punk band.
This is one angry guy and
I'm telling him that the publisher who
took his stuff is just a con
and then I read the poem about
my mother and sister
and hey, there's an act that's really lame!
Writing poems for your dead mother's approval.
But in spite of the brandy,
my flu,
my complete and utter inability to understand how to act
around people,
the crowd loves it, even better, they get it,
and as usual, nobody says dick to me after.
So I really ought to rethink
my strategy of using poetry to meet girls.
Because I go home alone
and I fall asleep
and dream about being lost.
Pursued by forces which intend to kill me.
It's Friday night in poet town.

Flying Under Duress

I wasn't ready to go.
I wasn't ready to die.
I wasn't ready to jump off of roofs.
I wasn't ready to be blown off a roof.
I was at work.
You understand, work!
This isn't life-threatening.
People don't die working the copier.
If the door opens there's a floor on the other side.
The worst thing about work is that it's boring.
Not frightening.
I mean except in a stupid way,
like your boss is mean,
or you don't get enough respect,
or the report's due tomorrow and the printer's all fucked up.
But that's it, you know?
Not frightening, not life threatening, not mangling,
not anything to worry about.
I mean I go to the top floor and check everything's nailed down.
It's just a double check,
like a checklist,
like making a list and checking it twice.
That doesn't kill you.
But I'm bending down and then the wind whips up and
this chunk of steel lifts me up and makes me like Superman
after the powers stop working.
For a second I'm airborne,
then I'm not,
then I'm racing to the ground and then I'm on it and then
I'm in it.

When I was fifteen, we read *Spoon River Anthology*
in High School English.
Bunch of stories of dead guys talking about themselves.
Now it's me talking and all I can think about is OSHA.
Forget the hard hat.
Forget the maximum load.
Forget everything but the harness.
I shouldn't have died.
I shouldn't have flown.
I should have been safe.
I should have been bored.
I should have been able to talk everyday,
drinking shitty coffee, to guys
who don't care about their jobs.
I should have been able to ignore my wife
and whatever dumb things she was saying.
I had a right to not look at my daughter
and whatever cute thing she was doing.
I didn't have to call my folks.
I should be alive.
I shouldn't ever have flown.

Letter to My Nieces on Their Birthdays

Good day to my favorite nieces.
All joy and luck to two wonderful young women.
This is a note from your uncle.
Your silly and foolish uncle.
You probably have never had anyone write you a poem.
May you have many more.
From young men who love you
and write passionately of your charms.
That will come.
But for now you'll have to take this as your gift.

I want to tell you about where you came from,
where you are, and where you can go.
You've spent your young lives in South Jersey,
like your parents, and their parents and like me for awhile.
You're two white girls in a world that is changing.
I'm an old man from a very different world.
When my father was young, he had negro maids
and cooks and a man brought milk each morning
in bright, glass containers.
Milk and cream and chocolate milk,
all fresh and pure and right from the farm.
He had a gardener come and trim the bushes.
He had a cook make everything they ate.
Roasts and turkeys and casseroles,
rich in cheese and meat and milk.
When I was young, we ate Thanksgiving Dinner
in the kitchen with the colored folk.

When I grew up, colored people could only
be janitors or porters on the railroad.
Now no one rides a railroad except as a treat.
I remember when I was ten, seeing young negro men
dancing to wild music and wishing I could dance like that.
They were up on a stage, legs all pumping, arms strong and wild
and I wanted to jump up and join them.
But I didn't.
It was South Jersey and you didn't do that in 1964.

The world spins, girls,
and changes all the time.
You have to be ready to spin and change with it.
You have to jump on the stage with the colored men
and dance with them.
You have to watch how the world spins and grab it
when you can.
It's easy to do just what the world expects.

When I was young, the world expected
you to hate negroes.
The world expected a black woman would clean your house.
That she would do it for next to nothing.
The world expected that you would grow up and get married
and have a couple of kids and love your children
and you would never have to work.
The world never expected women to work
or negros to have real jobs
or white folks to dance to negro music.

But that music has always been America's music
and it makes us dance.

The world is a wild dance
and you have to jump in.

The world isn't South Jersey.
The world isn't the USA.
The world is a wild mix
of horror and joy.

One day you'll fall in love.
Your heart will be an untamed beast
and you should never,
never,
tame that beast.
The beast made you.
The beast held you to its heart and said, I love you.
The beast mows your lawn
and cooks your dinner.
The beast watches you ride your bike and is terrified you'll die.
The beast is your parents and the beast is you.
Don't be scared.
Get up and dance.
Don't be afraid of what your friends say.
Don't worry about your grades.
Don't be stupid and listen to the voice that says,
what will my friends say?

The moon rises up tonight, wild and huge and it's asking you to dance.
Reach out and take its hand, my beautiful girls.
Dance across the lawn and feel your feet wet with dew.
And while you're dancing, think about me,
asleep and dreaming of girls dancing in the dew.

Mangoes and Rain

We go over and over the same ground.
I worry about the plants,
the warmer than usual spring,
the frost and the fall and the winter
and we start again.

We go for walks on the first nice day.
You say, how lovely.
My heart is racing.
We read and lie next to one another.
Argue over money or sex.
My lip jammed suddenly against my teeth.
There's a spot of blood.
There's a drop or two of cum.
A sigh.
I think about the yard.
How I'd like it to be.
You buy a picture at some store.
You know I'll hate it.
Did I ever get a gift I wanted?
There is summer and I eat fruit you've bought.
Kiss you once in a while.
Turn away from your breath, wipe my hand across my mouth.

Come home.
Come home.
Bring me fruit, even if it's bruised.
Let's eat the same food every day.
Just do it here.

Let this be the Spring where it's on fire.
Where the ice boils and
the taste in your mouth is mangoes and beer
and sour cream and
I can't seem to leave the house.
The tv blinks on then off all through the day.
It rains and rains and rains and there's no summer.
No fall.
No winter.
Just rain.
Strawberries,
soft with rot and juice
and you at the door always
coming home.
Your hair is wet.

The Receptionist

While I'm on the phone people come up and say hello.
They walk out front and grab a smoke.
They get in their cars and go off to appointments.
They gripe about traffic or like this one girl,
they gripe about how their car's fuel pump went
and I get to hear this long story about her driving
and maybe she's smoking in the car, listening to the radio.
She's driving and then the car sput, sputters and she says,
Oh no!
Not now!
But sure as shit the car stops right there in the middle of the road
and she's embarrassed and crying and then a guy comes to help her
and she comes into work and tells me all of this but
I hardly have time to listen, what with
the ringing of the phones
and jib jabbering of the customers
and the cheery hellos of the people I work with
and the loud honking from traffic down the road and
the roar in my head that won't be quiet.
Always having to be happy Jack.
Always having to listen to this jib, jib, jabber, this
constant nattering about cars and traffic and the talk radio
and the client being late or the customers too cheap
or the carpet looks awfully dirty, don't you think Jack?
And I think it does.
I think it's filthy.
I think it's covered in leaves and grit and old paper clips and
bits of shredded documents and torn newspaper.
I think I can't find the extension for the girl with the car thing.

The client is saying get me her boss and
the phones are ringing, ringing, ringing.
The cars are honking, honking, honking.
The clients are asking please, please.
The people are all outside smoking; they're all stuck in traffic.
There are thousands of them in the bright morning sun.
All waiting for the day to break over them like a dirty wave.
A wave filled with old tires, water bottles, dirty sneakers, plastic grocery
        bags,
paper coffee cups, all looming up gray and dirty and
then when it pulls away leaves the carpet filthy and familiar.
They wince from the brightness of the sun.
They turn away from how loud the sound of the radio can be.
They put their phones down.
They won't pick up.
They won't make their appointments.
They're waiting, waiting for the wave to go down.
But just behind it, there's another larger, dirtier, heavier wave
billowing up large and green and filled with all the rest of their lives
and it's all anyone can do to slump outside and
light up a smoke and
exhale in the crisp fall air.

PART IV

Misunderstood

She says, remember that time you climbed the water tower?
I said, what water tower? and she says, the one in your town.
But I never climbed the water tower and I was upset a little bit
because why would you bother climbing the water tower?
It was just big and green and went straight up and it wasn't all that tall.
But maybe I did climb it and I just didn't remember.
Although I don't think I would've told this woman,
I mean we'd just been arguing
over who wrote the lines about my hometown's name:
Wenonah.
I say, Longfellow and she says, Wordsworth
and I say, that's ridiculous
and she says, it is not; she says, it was a 19th century poet
and I get angry and say, why don't you just say some guy from the 1800's,
instead of being all pompous and saying 19th century?
Although I do know the line from the poem if not the poet,
"fair Nokomis bore a daughter and she called her name Wenonah..." and
only Longfellow could have written that sing-songy fake Indian (American, of
        course) junk
but for all I know, that's how Indians sound.
I mean, there were Indians when he was alive in 1888,
and he would have probably heard them talk and
they might actually talk in some odd meter that would sound
like a drum beat
but a dumb drumbeat with rhymes and other 19th century constructions and
maybe they really wore headdresses made of feathers,
maybe photographers didn't pull one out of a closet and
put them on and say, okay, look noble and stuff.
So, if I'm wrong about the meter and I can't remember if in 1988 it's the
        20th century,

then maybe it really is Wordsworth that wrote Hiawatha.

That could be right.

Henry Wordsworth.

But I'm certain it's Henry Wadsworth Longfellow,

the American poet of the 19th century

whose poem, Hiawatha, was a best seller and

was singlehandedly responsible for dozens of developments all over a

      newly middle class USA being named Wenonah.

I read Hiawatha so I know I'm right, although maybe

I didn't read it.

Maybe I just looked at it in a book,

it being old and dull and sing-songy and fake Indian

by a man with three names in the 1800's,

because I was at an art exhibit by painters of the 19th century,

American Landscape Painters of the 19th Century.

And one of their big topics was Hiawatha and

there were like 4 paintings of this one battle

between some Indian and some monster and

I didn't even remember the monster.

I don't have the vaguest idea what the fuck Hiawatha was doing in the

      poem.

All I can remember really is his mom having a baby named Wenonah or

maybe it's his grandmother having his mother and

then they build a development on a creek in southern NJ

next to a town called Mantua, for God's sake, after

the Italian Mantua of the 16th century or whatever,

really a long time ago you know,

and call it Wenonah and at a certain point they need water and

build this tower on the highest hill and

there aren't many hills, trust me, and

fill it with water and it's cheaper to pump it and

sometime in the mid 20th century when I'm stoned on pot with two other

      nincompoops,

I climb it.
Then for some reason, which I can't figure, I tell this woman about climbing it.
Then she remembers it and spits this memory back at me ten years later
when I'm a little drunk and I'm thinking she used to be cuter and I'm
looking over her shoulder at a cuter woman maybe ten years younger
at this party in New Hampshire in the 21st century.
The 21st century!!
I honestly don't think I ever climbed that tower.
I think she's confused.
I think she wishes I did.
I think Longfellow wrote Hiawatha.
I think Wordsworth was probably a better poet.
I think I'm not going to fuck this girl and that it's a no brainer.
But I can't get it out of my mind.

I'm on top of the tower.
I'm turning around and
around under the turning heavens.
It's the end of the 20th century
and I'm drunk on possibility.
It could have happened.
Maybe it did.
Maybe it should have.

Cleaning House

I can't write about love.
That's a sad joke.
Last October I came this close
to dying of love or something like it.
HIV, AIDS, Wasting,
call it what you want
but it left me here
and now I can't write.
Not about love or what my friend Lisa
calls my personal doom.
Because, after all, how many ways
can you say I'm dying?
Just one and just once.
Because I was dying, my brothers brought me here.
To the town where I grew up.
This town with its trees,
its families, its planters hanging on porches,
swinging slow in the humid evenings.
I don't know what to say about it.
I'm not angry, I'm alive after all and
it's a sweet town and the people all smile
but why they smile and how and when I can't say.
Because all I can remember is what was here before.

This was my home.
Its park in the center, its railroad trestle,
the swamps on the edge of town,
the cupolas, the gingerbread, the dark windows,
the cry of birds, the hiss of rain.

The girls I dated all lived here.
The cars I drove went up and down these streets.
The high school, the gravel schoolyard,
the cold beers, the hay on the knees of my pants,
the slow stream running through the swamp and
lilacs.
The fights with my brothers.
The agonies of every dumb kid played out every day.
The mad walks out of town crying because of some stupid thing.
My mother chasing me in the car saying, "It will be all right."
Girls and sex and erections and the odd smell
of my first ejaculation and hiding my underwear from my mother.
Why would I do that?
All these thoughts press in around me every night.
Ghosts watching me sleeping, leering at the
sad erections I get in my sleep.
This place is too much of my past.
This God damned house.
This house my brothers made for me.
The bed they smoothed for me, the shades pulled down waiting for me,
the floors they cleaned while I lay in the hospital, all nice and neat and
ready in this fussy house.
This house I lie in night after night waiting
for my personal doom in this crappy town
with all it's lousy, happy people,
walking brightly down the street.
Laughing people, dreaming dreams that you don't hide.
Happy people in a haunted house.

It's a sunny day in this shithole.
It's day time and nobody but me sees the ghosts.
The shit smeared on the floors from the man who

sits on the toilet filled with shame.
Nobody sees my brothers mopping, cleaning,
pulling the shades, worried, waiting for my doom.
Who could write about this?
Who would write about this?
A man asleep in a clean bed, covers pulled up,
a man with a smile on his sleeping face.
A man who dreams a vivid dream and wakes up hard as a rock.

Poem about Food

Loaves, fishes, desire, joy, eating,
eating, eating, 40 loaves, 40 fishes, eating,
drinking wine spodee o dee, drinking wine.
Saving the good for last.
The joy of drinking the last drop from the last jug.
The sopping of butter from the fishes.
The loaf crunchy and stale and hearty and what's in it?
How good could it taste with that wine we had last week at the wedding?
The last drop. Good.
The fish, was it haddock? Was it sturgeon? Was that roe on top? Was that
butter browned or compound?
The wine, the loaf, the fish, the bread crispy, not at all stale.
Perfect semolina even here in the desert and nowhere a mention of death,
just food, just wine, and food and dry turkey or dry wine or dry bread but
rich and glowing and needed.
Like if you had to eat.
Had to or you'd die.
You'd eat, you say but I say, you might not.
You might choose another way.
You might vomit or starve. I say, you might not eat.
I didn't, now I do.
Bread and wine and fishes.
Enough for a long time.

Giving Up The Ghost

I live in Jersey City
in a condo in a building
formerly gutted by fire.
When my old boss did the
termite inspection, the basement
was filled with rats.
My wife and I were the only
residents for a long time.
Each night I heard a young girl sobbing.
It was home to crackheads and worse.
I'm not certain all the spirits
here have my best interests at heart.
So I'm casting them out.
I'm asking their forgiveness
for fucking with their
foolish sorrow.
Their stupid anger.
Ghosts! Listen up!
Life is joy and sorrow all mixed up.
Like the food on your plate at a glorious Thanksgiving.
Olives and peas and cranberry
all shoving and pushing for your attention.
But you're hoisting glass after glass
of the most wonderful red wine
and laughing till you cry
and taking another huge forkful
of food and you barely notice
how lucky you are to have it.
The olives soaked in oil and pepper.

The peas, small and sweet and silly
because your Aunt Gert made them every year.
The cranberry bright with orange zest
and rum and Kenny nearly crying about
that snowy Thanksgiving on E. 12 St. in 1989.
Goodbye, my sweet little ghosts.
Sleep tight, my poor little girl.
I'll be going now.
I'll leave you to your rats and this old city,
tucked up on a cold cliff in late 1997.

Pilgrimage

I go with my friend Jane to
Jimmy's Downtown in midtown for dinner.
It's early September and a nice warm evening.
We walk a bit and do that
New York thing of figuring out how to
get a cab at 5:30. There's not much traffic
and everyone's walking with
purpose
like always in New York and
Jane buys cigarettes and bitches
that for seven fifty she should get matches and
our cabbie, some Indian guy, is smart and
gets us to 55th street with a minimum of fuss.
We get cocktails and I smoke a cigar.
I bought it on 18th from some Dominican.
Then we start with dinner and
because my old girlfriend Linda is the chef
we get the tasting menu.
Bread with aromatic oils:
orange, pepper, rosemary.
Scallops and crab.
Tender chicken and corn and lamb and
steak and sturgeon and dessert.
The tables around us fill up along with our bellies.
A group of office-workers, two black women,
an Asian lady, three Spanish men, a white guy.
We're sure the guy two tables over is famous.
We meet the owner, Jimmy, and I schmooze him
and tell him what a great restaurant he has and

what a great chef Linda is and
then we leave to go home.
But we don't.
This is New York on a beautiful Friday night.
So we go downtown to Wall St. to Jane's favorite bar
and on the way, a block from Trinity Church,
I see all the lights from 1 and 2 World Trade.
Which aren't there.
Are gone, really.
We get to the bar and drink and talk to the regulars.
All of them drunk by now like us.
Anyway, I'm arguing with a bunch of drunks about my poetry
and a young girl, not a regular but still very drunk, flirts with me.
For the first time in a year,
somebody finds me attractive.
I'm really glad because two weeks
after the eleventh of September,
I got really sick and almost died
and for most of the past year,
I looked like a skeleton
and clacked around like one and
never imagined I could end up drunk
three days before the second 9/11 flirting with a girl,
drunk, full of food and New York.
Hell, I thought I'd be dead.
When I was really sick, I watched hour after hour
of TV news about New York and
the armies of Afghanistan and happy families and
dreamed at night about Satan
and Michael the Archangel battling for my soul.
Now, having been restored to this world,
I've found all this glee two blocks from Hell.

That's got to mean something, don't you think?
The next day having stumbled into my friend's home at 4:30 AM,
I wake up at 8:30 AM and go to help Linda, the chef, my ex,
fix her computer and her heart
which has been broken by two other guys.
Which is not to say I didn't have a hand in it.
I did, long ago.
Only that she needed help and
then I went back to my friend's and after waking up
later that afternoon, still tired,
I saw the great procession of the Feast of the Martiri de Dio
wind by their home,
accompanied by the sad bleating of a ragged band and
boys in badly fitted white robes and clerics and
the children and grandchildren and great grandchildren of the
town of Molfetta, Italy and two great statues
pass me by.
It might have been 1802.
They sang a hymn in Italian.
A white balloon soared up and across the street.
A blessing.
I was tired.
I was hung over.
I was a worn out battleground.
It's my recollection that the Red Cross
was founded when tourists in the 1850's
in Italy, coming down from the Alps,
stumbled on the site of recent battle in some war.
They didn't even know about the war.
Vultures and thieves were picking over the dead and wounded.
Men were still alive and screaming
in the crisp fall air and no one

was there to offer aid.
They watched for a time and moved on,
finishing the day with a rich meal
in an inn known for its hospitality
and gracious surroundings.
I passed by the town in which I lived and nearly died.
I ate well.
I drank well.
I nodded my head at a sacred site
and when I returned, I slept.
Well.

Poem for the Soon to Die

Shut up about cancer.
Uteran, breast, testicular, pancreatic,
metastatic, benign, blighted monster
lying in bed with your mother.
Shut up about it.
Shut up about your funeral.
Get buried in your flannel nightie
with the names of your grandchildren
and the bunny ear slippers
or get burned up, but however you do it:
three days at the wake,
open casket,
headstone,
beloved wife long remembered
lo, these many years mouldering,
keep it to yourself.
It's not for me.
The big faceless statues,
the candles at the shop of Mickey Morales,
gunned down at 46; everybody loved him.
Can the sappy, war dead poems,
Joyce Kilmer, Edward Thomas, Wilfred Owen,
the dead are dead—so fuck them.
We're alive.
Let's act like it.
Don't plan your dying.
Live.

The Exterminator's Call

I'm waiting for the exterminator to call.
I've called three times and he hasn't returned the call.
I've told him it's urgent
or rather left a message saying, "It's urgent."
But he hasn't returned the call.
I can see the termites in one of the support timbers.
If you poke it with a screwdriver, they come spilling out,
a thousand tiny white bodies.

I haven't had sex in nearly a year.
I couldn't masturbate until two months ago and
even then, I have to wait two, three days to gather
the energy to come.
I haven't been drunk but the one time in nearly a year,
or done drugs, or held another person close to say
I love you.

But I read a good deal.
Mysteries and biographies and the stories of powerful forces.
The building of New York City.
The killing of a black judge in a room in DC.
The machinations of Lyndon Baines Johnson as he struggles
to pass a civil rights bill in 1956.
Erotic stories by my friend, Tsaurah, an older woman with a very
dirty mind.

The IRS has decided my debts are uncollectible.
Women walk by my house, sweaty in the evening heat, exercising.
They're housewives.

I eat corn and grill ribs and wait for the exterminator to return my call.
I send angry emails to him.
No response.
Each night at 6, I see a cardinal flash across the yard.
People try to tell me about Jesus.
The bible, salvation, redemption, going to heaven.

I tell them I don't care about heaven.
I'm more interested in that cardinal.
In the call from the exterminator.
I'm more interested in my daily swim in the lake.
Cool brown water. They call it cedar water here.
It stains your skin brown.
I swim slow because of my recent illness and watch the
hawks circle across the way.
There are snapping turtles lined up on a log a few yards from where I swim.
The children warn me about them.
Look out for the snapping turtles.
Every other night or so the heat gives way to hot lightning.
A crack and flash a few times.
The humidity doesn't break, the exterminator doesn't call,
the turtles sit fat and happy on their log and the children
are afraid.
As they should be.
All these debts are uncollectible.

Losing

My friend Danny lost his mother a year ago.
She wasn't the best mother in the world,
but she was Danny's.
Danny's mother had a son who died in Dachau
or Auschwitz.
It doesn't matter.
A lot of Jews died and with them their world.
Parlors filled with brilliant guests, rich pastries,
conversations and argument.
All gone.
But Danny's mother lucks out,
sort of, and comes to America
and marries and gives birth to two sisters and Danny.
One sister doesn't work out well and
spends the rest of her life in institutions.
Even Danny's mother does badly.
So Danny's other sister is kind of like
his mother.
Her name is Carol.
She and her husband,
Leo,
raise up Danny.
It's like medicine.
It's like a miracle.
It's like love.
So Carol and Leo and Danny are here in America.
There are no brilliant parlors.
There is no dense, rich pastry.
There is only

Carol, too young, raising Danny
in Dumont, Bergen County, New Jersey, and
there is a joy no one can really acknowledge.
My sister hates my father because
he was fucking my stepmother
as my mother was dying.
I'm watching a special on diabetes.
Children were starved to prevent disease.
Stacked in graves thin as rails.
Today, Danny's sister Carol left her husband Leo.
His other sister sits in an asylum.
He has no mother.
No sister.
No brother.
No father.
They're all dead.
Tell me how to see that
God.
You lousy son of a bitch.
Carol is happy,
maybe,
Leo is happy,
maybe,
Danny is lost,
always.
My mother has always been dead,
like my friend's brother.
Death is not a friend or a brother or a sister.
It wakes up tired and sad
and it goes to work.
It has a job and we're its simple acquaintances.

New Year's Eve

I go out on New Year's Eve. I hate New Year's Eve but it's the year 2000 and so I have to go out and have fun so I go to my friend Linda's house and Linda serves a good meal, tarts and roasts and rack of lamb and Linda's sister Pattie brings wine and the wine is equal to the meal. Light, airy whites, thick, rich reds, and finally a dessert wine, a German wine, slick and sugary and this isn't a bad way to come to the next century, I think but there's more to do. I'm invited to another party to ring in the new, so I say goodbye and everyone's mad at me, no surprise there, and I go to Danny and Caroline's for music and drink. Danny and Caroline's is filled with children. Children and parents of children and there is music but there is also parents yelling at children and children saying please, please, please. But there is also wine and I'm happy for that and there is talk with good friends and that's not bad and there's this guy holding forth and smoking tons of cigarettes and Caroline says that's my friend Mike Latch and we talk for a good while and this guy is wired up like some junior Neal Cassady and we're drinking red wine from Bulgaria, bulls blood, and the cigarettes are everywhere. Then he reads Rimbaud for the millennium, then there are fireworks everywhere and the sky is filled with red and white and green flowers and it's officially the next day, next month, next year, next century and I feel good that I didn't do anything wrong for once but just eat and drink and talk with my friends on a night not so strange, except for red filling the sky.

What I Learned When I Was Sick

That you can die.
That all the medicine in the world
might prove inadequate
and if it does, you die.

I learned how to live with
yourself when you shit your pants
and that it's a good idea to
have a portable toilet.
I learned that being really sick
smells like being very young
and that you can go for days
without sleep.
I learned you have to wait.
Some things take a long time
and they take that long
no matter what.
I learned I like to
work and that I like a clean house
and that you should
not walk at night with
your hands in your pockets
and that if you are so foolish
as to go for a walk on a
frigid January night,
whatever you do don't look
up at the stars.
I learned you might trip.
I learned because trip I did.

My skull smacking the cold
concrete.
WHAM!
Just like that!
So watch where you're going.
Don't look back.
Death is just behind you
all the time,
like a friend who walks
just a little slower
and one day you're on the
corner looking up at the light
waiting to cross
and he reaches out & touches you.
Soft but final.

The Poem Where I Say Thank You

You know, it's really not that bad that I get paid
two fifty an hour for work that needs to be done.
Work I would do for free.
Work that needs to be done.
Like a farmer who has a second job so he can afford
to bring in the hay each summer.
Like a painter who labors as a printer
then goes home to some dirty loft,
paints for five hours,
alone,
to make something people might never see.
It's not the money.
It's not job advancement.
It's the accretion of paint,
the tufts of hay glowing in the late summer,
the roar of the tractor,
the shouts of the boy in the back of the truck.
It's the great deep gulp of water after hours of hard work.
It's the mumbled gasp of awe when a friend
walks into the studio and says,
Oh, my God.
Oh, my God.

We go to work.
We buy our coffee in paper cups and pour in cream.
We want to do well and
we get frustrated when we fail.
But we still have the loft.
We still have the field.

The field our father left us.
The farm eaten by subdivisions so all that is left
is six small acres and
only my brother cares about the farm.
He still gets up at five and
trudges out in his boots
to see to the cows and the pigs and the scraggly chickens
and when he tells people at work he's a farmer they laugh.
A farmer.

Why do you get up early to feed the stupid pigs and
come home late to plow the land and
ask the boss for a couple days off at haying time and
he says, haying time, what the fuck is that?
What indeed.

What about the crisp smell of turpentine and oil?
What about the rasp of knife on canvas?
What about the question of white?
What about the happy rush of pigs to the trough,
the satisfying turn of plow through earth?
The deep smell of things long buried?
Who else knows and who else cares and still
you take up brush and knife and cleaver and plow.
Dig deep in the earth and work and work
and think this is it.
This is it?

Oh, but my friend this is it!
This is the glorious rush of fruition!
This is harvest.
This is pumpkins dotting the soil everywhere.

Potatoes spilling up out of the ground like angry bones.
This is ugly red and awkward gesso and the spread of manure.
This is the man with dirty boots walking at 5 AM
in a field in South Jersey saying, what the fuck am I doing?
This is our job.
The housewife rising at 6 to put the sandwiches in the bags
for lunch for the kids that are so sick of peanut butter and jelly,
they'd kill for bologna.
This is the mechanic, sick with a hangover,
sliding under an engine at 7 AM
that's got to be ready for some old guy by 9 and
you think he could wait, at least a little.
This is the girl in the WaWa filling urn after urn of okay coffee
for league upon league of men in dirty boots
spilling out of pick up after pick up after pick up.
She says, last night my daughter and
I made a mountain out of paste for her project.
It was a map of the universe and
I didn't even know where Wanaque was.
But there it was, right where my father grew up.
Right next to the factory where he worked for
twenty odd years till he had sense enough to move.
Who works?
Who paints?
Who are we?

People who farm.
People who work.
People with courage and kids and
jobs that pay okay and
at least I have benefits and
I think every day I wake up that it's a blessing

I have today.
A blessing.

So the farmer turns under the crop.
So the painter smears white over everything and starts again.
So you get up and take a shower and drink your coffee and kiss the
wife and think your kids are ungrateful but then on the way to work
you notice the way the air smells today.
You see the golden tinge of sun on the fields you drive by every day.
You notice the brief brush of clouds over the sun and the fog hugging
the deep places on the back roads and you say, maybe, maybe
it's a blessing.

PART V

The Night My Old Lover Comes to Tell Me of Her Wedding

My friend Jessica asks me if I've read about
the murders in Algeria.
Guys break into houses and kill
everyone at home.
Sometimes they rape the women.
I say, yeah, I saw it on 60 Minutes.
I say, it's crazy.
What's the point?
Jessica and my friend Andy, who's with us,
say everybody in Algeria gets the point.
The veil, the dietary laws, the proper way
to honor God.

Andy tells us both about having sex
while reading WR.
He was with a woman he loved.
He says they levitated.
He clearly believes it.
Two days later he tries the same trick
with the wife of an itinerant house painter.
He shoves the guy's paint cans out of the way and
fucks her on the floor of the guy's van.
Nothing.
No rise. Not even an inch or two.
He concludes love is the operating principle.

I love Jessica with a hurt so hard
it feels like the pull of gravity.

When she kisses me goodbye,
she really means goodbye.
Swarms of Algerians storm the doors,
slit my throat,
and leave me to bleed to death.
It is a right and fitting way to honor the Lord.
I am rising.

I'm a Tourist

I get on a boat,
a sailboat,
with several people I've never met before and
a woman who's asked me to come.
A friend,
someone who wants to be my lover.
We go out into the harbor of New York.

It's night.
Sail boats move across the water without noise
and we move over the water like that.
Quiet.
We move across a place I've never been.
Across water I've always seen and have never seen.
The Hudson.
We brush against little islands two feet wide.
No one knows why they're there.

I land in Macedonia,
a little country in the Balkans.
I flew in a tiny Russian jet filled with Albanians.
They're happy to go home to a place that booted them out.
There is nothing there.
Just farms and falling down concrete buildings
and old, old, old buildings.

I'm there on business.
I meet my business associates very late.
They're glad to see me.
The Albanians on the plane with me are happy to be here.

The river that runs through the capital of Macedonia
is named for water.
The brandy we drink is named water.
Vodka.
We drink as though there would never be water again.
We show our product to a hundred people
in a hundred hotel rooms.
We drink brandy.
We eat.

I feel like I'm home but I'm not.
I lay in bed in my hotel room
and I'm sad.
No one knows me here.
But when I arrived, I saw
farms
and highways,
and when we drive the highways,
we pass carts drawn by horses.
Gypsies,
my friends say.
The gypsies live by the dumps.

In the harbor our boat passes oil refineries
and docks filled with BMWs
and my friend brushes her legs against me
and I can't return her desire.
I can only look up at the great Verrazano,
the deep, dark green of Staten Island.
I'm stuck in a silent boat flying over a deep river
with islands so small no one knows them.

The country of Macedonia
has a lake so big everyone goes there.
Ohrid.
Black.
Every woman in Macedonia is beautiful and
none of them speak English.
I'm an American walking streets so old
only the Turks remember building them.
We walk into the Ministry of Defense.
It looks like a rotting insane asylum.

We drink brandy.
We walk down streets and talk about business.
We go out one night to the amusement park
in the center of town.
Every young person in town is here to
meet every other young person in town
and they're all beautiful and they all want to go to America.
We go to a bar where they play the music of my youth.
Creedence.
The Dead.
Every one is drinking vodka.
Water.
The river bed is wide but runs with a trickle of water.

In the harbor of New York,
it is deep with water.
It is water filled with the stars and the moon and the
debris of all the old tenements.
The islands we pass were built of discarded tenements.
The brick and mortar and facades of asylums
and capitols and dead Dutchmen.

I'm a tourist in a boat.
I ride a quiet wind gliding over waves.
A woman strokes my legs
and I want to leave.
I can't.
I can't shake the tide, the water, the drinks,
the cement deep under the water.

I want to get up from the boat.
I want to go home.
I want the light of the giant statue in the harbor to
go out so I can go home.
So I can go anywhere but here
and eat food I've never eaten.
But all the food everywhere is the same
and everyone washes it down with water.
Water like brandy.
Water that makes concrete.
Water that hides what we need.
I'm thirsty; I'm in Europe.
I'm a tired tourist in a Ministry of Defense
in a country that can't hold it's liquor.
It's quiet.
It's water.
It's a light from a statue, from stars, from the miniature golf course
in the middle of town filled with girls and boys playing at love.
We're all going to go home
and when we get here, we're thirsty
and there's not enough water
to quench our thirst.
We're always going home.
We're always on the water.
We're always tourists.

Oceans and Stars

I sleep, though not well, getting up to
piss throughout the night.
Late, after 3 AM, while I'm pissing, I can see stars.

The stars are in the heavens for a reason.
To help sailors on their way.
They guide boats across the deep, deep sea.
They're signs.
They're way points.
They're something solid and safe for a man
alone on the ocean in a tiny boat.
In the ocean, you could be hundreds of miles from land.
Your ship could be small,
just a few timbers and a sail.
Your ship will be wet because ships are never dry, not ships of wood.
They carry the ocean in their hull.
They carry the threat of drowning just below your feet.
Insects eat your ship, gnaw at the damp wood, encourage
the ocean to join them.
The ocean seeks itself, through your ship's hull,
over the sides, slopping just under your feet.

Above you, the stars say:
this way,
this way.
While you're looking up,
the ocean is coming home.
While you stand over the side pissing your life away,
your piss washes back up over your shoes.

Your piss seeps in past the weevils and the worms to
sit warm and wet at the bottom of your boat.
The stink of the hold, the warm water sloshing
over hard tack and stores, is safe below the deck.
You hardly notice the slow rot of your life.
The disease waiting to claim you.
The long night, full of stars, claims you instead.
You look up to the stars, never down at the sea.
You're soon to drown in your own piss.

NOISE

Kids arguing outside my window.
My landlord's whores screaming, Ray, Ray,
while I try to sleep.
It's 5 AM; don't they give a shit about anybody?
They've been up all night sniffing junk and smoking crack
and now it's time to sleep
and they're yelling and yelling and yelling.
And all this racket, this godawful racket.

A man calls to ask about my attendance at a conference.
He asks when I'll be flying in.
I'm dumbfounded for a minute.
I won't be flying in, not now anyway.
Maybe not ever.
Maybe I don't care about talking
to chemical distributors about GPS.
My voice starts to rise in anger.
Righteous, righteous anger.

A friend asks me to go to a reading.
A poetry reading.
People talking about their problems,
trivializing the trivial.
I'm suddenly sad.
I wanted to go to her reading.
She's a good poet and I like to hear
her words and I know several others
performing with her.
I like their work as well

but for me it would be like,
I don't know, like hearing someone talking to you,
but you're thinking of something else,
like the death of your mother so many years ago.
Or a pigeon wobbling on the side of a building across the street.
It's sick; it's going to fall.

An old lady wheels her shopping cart down the street.
It squeals and it squeals and each squeal is terrible.
I want it to stop.
There's a dog barking a block away and it just barks
and barks and barks.
It barks because it can.
Because it's angry, because it's hurt.
I want to grab the cart and smash it.
I want to push the dog from the fence.
I want to say, can't you hear that noise?
I want to stroke it's rough fur and murmur,
can't you hear?
Shush, be quiet, shush, be quiet.

On Tuesday I watched the most horrible things
I've ever seen or expected to see.
All in quiet.
I'm reading the papers day after day
and the pictures are still.
Still pictures.
Two immense buildings implode.
Thousands die.
In silence.
It's a racket that gets so loud,
it's all you can do to stop hearing, stop listening.

Praying for Rest

I was dead
but doctors saved me,
lifted me up and put me back in the world.
Now I hardly sleep.
I watch TV.
CNN, MSNBC, NBC,
the news, the war, the weather,
the TV.
I watch the TV morning, noon, and night.
It's not death.
It's TV. It's always on.
I'm always up, taking medicine,
drinking water,
taking great gulps of life.
It hasn't rained is what I hear on the TV.
It's dry.
It's an arctic air mass stalled.
It's eighty unburied bodies in Georgia.
Wake them up.
Raise them in their gory shrouds,
stitch up their gaping mouths and show them TV.
Show them the rain.
Ask if it hurts.
Ask if the lawn filled with crocuses
in February is risen or doomed.
Ask them to pray for rain, for me.
Forgiven.

Why Ask Why

Think of my sister as a cake
and my mother as a chef and
a not very good one.
Working year in, year out,
at a respectable place.
Once very good,
now only okay and only the regulars come back.
But still, there is silver on the tables,
nice china
covering the occasional worn spot
on the cloth and even though
the food rarely surprises, it's rich
in spice and memories and
every once in a while, the soufflé is dazzling.
The waiter beaming.
The night perfect, so you know
why she still unwraps her knives
every night, because magic is still
a possibility.
But my sister came out all wrong.
Before the salad, after the coffee
and Mrs. Hurine is sitting stiff at her table.
The tip is very small.
So my mother carefully cleaned
and wrapped her knives
in their black leather case and
quietly resigned.
Then she went away to cry.

But my sister isn't an egg, or a soufflé, or a cake
and my mother couldn't bear it.
So she went into a little hospital,
all slathered in white stucco.
A doctor gave her an epidural and pulled out
Mary Louise and because my mother
couldn't stop her foolish crying,
which shouldn't have been a disaster,
anymore than a poorly plated quail is a disaster.
After all, chefs love to cook and customers love to eat
and food is food, no matter when it comes out.
So my brother and I ate rich, perfect lasagna
at Mrs Paolo's every day for a month.
We got lost in pasta and gravy and thin veal
sweet as sugar and the deep bite of garlic.
And so today,
when my brother asks what happened
when my sister was born,
was our mother home?
I take a bite of salad and a sip of zinfandel
and say,
she was nuts.
They locked her up and for one month
we ate like little princes.

The Taste of Beer in Late Fall

I need to talk to my brother now.
I need to tell him
my house is clean.
I fixed the broken chest
of drawers. I need to tell
him about the Palisades.
The Hoboken Library, a Tuscan
ruin in a pale, pink dawn.
I need to tell him
I'm falling in love.
That trees have been stripped
of their leaves after a hard
cold rain.
That I've been on my knees
scrubbing.
Tears at my throat nearly every day
and I need to tell him I'm sitting
alone in this clean house
waiting.
My heart beating so loud
it fills the room.
I'm waiting.
He needs to know.
I need to tell.

Back to Work

Just so you know, I'm back
at Acme Exterminating Company
on Ninth Avenue in New York.
The rug in the office is the one
I had installed in 1994.
I got a good deal on that rug, so good,
that they've never gotten
new carpeting, even though
it looks like shit and all.
The people in the office are the same.
Same desks and chairs and stairs and owner.
Some horrible museum of my life.
Like the kid who smacks the family Buick
into a tree and dies and his parents
leave his room exactly how it was.
Metallica poster, NFL sheets,
skate punk magazines in a box under the bed.
The windows never opened. No one lives there.
The shades always drawn.
The room clean for the first time ever and always clean forever.
The socks in order.
T-shirts faded. The parents walk in and
sob for a second.
Never together.
Never touching anything.
Except to dust and smooth the sheets.

That's my job.
I'm Tom Sawyer watching my own funeral.

Only, Becky Thatcher walks in every day and
says, "Tom, you shithead."
And the whole town chimes in with a litany of shortcomings.
He was drunk; he took dope; he abandoned us!
He was a stupid piece of shit and we're still here.

I should be mad but secretly
I'm flattered they even show up.
So I bow my head,
open my desk and go to work.

Astrology in the Year 2003

I live in a town where you can see the stars.
Where I can tell it's December because
my beloved Orion twirls above my house.
Where I can imagine all my friends born in December
to be full of drink and bluster and luck
and perhaps leaning
over towards someone in a bar
to tell them how important it is to live
to really live
and of course they have all of twelve dollars
in their pockets but they're in New York City.
A city that always has Orion twirling overhead.

My friend Linda writes about how angry she is
with the world.
With George Bush and his band of cronies and
the collapse of kindness and the bodies in
the passes of the Hindu Kush.
Me too.
Except I sat in the Campbell Bar
in Grand Central Station
and listened to Caroline tell me about Henry IV on Broadway
and Hotspur and Falstaff and the actors' spit flying six rows out
and my drink, old whiskey, and this city, this theater, this bar, this
brief flirtation.

Fuck George Bush.
Fuck everyone who can't
sit on their porch with a glass and imagine the cold winter

to come and fuck people who can't imagine
the angel of death at their door.
Fuck them for opening the door.
Fuck them for not leaning back against the porch rail,
for not pushing back their chair at the bar on this first
cold night of December.
Yes! It's the Angel of Death at your door!
Who else?
And behind her Spring and Summer and Erato and Desire and
just past that, the Stars.
Winking.
Winking.
Whispering in your ear
in the Campbell Bar in the Grand Central Station
with it's angel on the roof, it's
rails running to the far corners of this world
and she's saying, "Take my hand.
Let's walk out under the stars,"
and she says it every December, just as I grow older.
And I take her hand
and lead her out and
I show her the sky in my town!

The Names of God

I dreamed the other night about dogs.
In the dream, I was hired to rid a school of some pests.
When I arrived at the school,
I entered a classroom and it was full of dogs.
That's the name of God.

I had another dream.
I was sleeping in a room with several other people.
The young girl next to me reached over and stroked my penis.
That was the name of God.

My porch is littered with dead blossoms from the flowers I've planted.
Each blossom is one of God's names.
Each time I walk past them, I hear a quiet murmur.
I eat quickly and neglect my friends.
I sleep fitfully.
Behind the caterwauling and clutter,
I hear the quiet whisper of God's name.

It's not something you want to hear.
It's literature left on the porch from 7th Day Adventists.
It's a half eaten dinner.
It's wine turned sour sitting in the sun.
Then sometimes it announces itself loud and without ambiguity.
We can tell when that happens.
Say when your child is born
or when a great man is struck down or
a storm carries away a whole world.
Those names of God we all know.

It's the other names that cause us concern and distress.
We know we hear them;
we know we should attend,
but it's late and we're tired.
We'd like to hold our loved ones close and
shut out the noise of the world.
But it's God's world and it's His noise and it never stops.
It would be sweet if all of God's names were names we knew.
It would be sweet.

CAVANKERRY'S MISSION

Through publishing and programming, CavanKerry Press connects communities of writers with communities of readers. We publish poetry that reaches from the page to include the reader, by the finest new and established contemporary writers. Our programming brings our books and our poets to people where they live, cultivating new audiences and nourishing established ones.

OTHER BOOKS IN THE NOTABLE VOICES SERIES